KRAKOW TRAV
2023

Discover the Best of Krakow, Poland

Steve Kaswui

Rights Reserved.

TABLE OF CONTENTS

Welcome To Krakow

Grace had always been fascinated by history and had a particular interest in World War II. When she had the opportunity to visit Krakow, a city that held significant historical importance, he eagerly packed his bags and set off on his journey.

As Grace arrived in Krakow, she was immediately struck by the city's vibrant atmosphere. The old town's cobblestone streets were lined with colorful buildings, and the rhythmic clatter of horse-drawn carriages filled the air. It was like stepping back in time.

Her first stop was the famous Wawel Castle, a magnificent fortress that stood tall atop a hill. As Grace explored the castle's grounds, she couldn't help but imagine the grandeur of the Polish kings who once resided there. The castle's majestic architecture and stunning views of the Vistula River left him in awe.

Next, Grace visited the historic Jewish quarter, Kazimierz. Walking through its narrow streets, she felt a mix of melancholy and admiration. The quarter had once been a vibrant center of Jewish culture before the tragedy of the Holocaust. Grace visited the Galicia Jewish Museum, which beautifully documented the history and heritage of the Jewish community in the region. The exhibitions were both informative and emotionally moving, reminding Grace of the importance of preserving and learning from the past.

One of the highlights of Grace's visit was a trip to Auschwitz-Birkenau, the infamous Nazi concentration camp. As she stepped onto the grounds, she was overwhelmed by the weight of history. Walking through the barracks and seeing the remnants of the gas chambers, Grace couldn't help but feel a deep sense of sorrow and empathy for the victims. It was a haunting experience that left a lasting impact on his perspective of the world.

Despite the somber moments, Krakow offered moments of joy and celebration as well. Grace immersed herself in the city's vibrant culture and sampled delicious Polish cuisine. She indulged in pierogies, savory dumplings filled with various ingredients, and sipped on traditional Polish vodka, toasting to the warmth and hospitality of the Polish people.

Grace also had the opportunity to witness the lively festivities during the Krakow International Folklore Festival. The streets came alive with music, dance, and colorful costumes from different cultures around the world. The energy and enthusiasm of the performers and spectators were infectious, creating a memorable and joyous atmosphere.

As Grace's visit to Krakow came to an end, she couldn't help but reflect on the incredible history she had encountered. The city had been through dark times, but it had also risen from the ashes, embracing its past while looking towards the future. The resilience of the Polish people and their commitment to preserving their heritage left a deep impression on her.

As she boarded her flight back home, Grace carried with her not only memories but also a newfound appreciation for the importance of understanding history. Krakow had opened her eyes to the power of remembrance and the necessity of learning from the past to build a better future.

Krakow had become more than just a tourist destination for Grace; it had become a place of profound learning and personal growth. She knew that the impact of her visit would stay with her for a lifetime, inspiring her to continue exploring history and sharing its lessons with others.

CHAPTER 1: INTRODUCTION

Krakow's Brief History

Krakow, located in southern Poland, is a city steeped in rich history and cultural heritage. Its origins can be traced back to the 7th century when it was established as a settlement on the banks of the Vistula River. Over the centuries, Krakow grew in importance, becoming the capital of Poland in the 11th century and serving as the seat of Polish kings for many years.

During the medieval period, Krakow flourished as a center of trade and intellectual activity. It attracted merchants from all over Europe and became a melting pot of cultures and ideas. The city's architectural wonders, such as the iconic Wawel Castle and the magnificent St.

Mary's Basilica, were constructed during this era, showcasing the wealth and power of the Polish kingdom.

In the 16th century, Krakow experienced a period of decline as the capital was moved to Warsaw. However, the city continued to be a cultural and intellectual hub, with the establishment of the Jagiellonian University in 1364. The university became a renowned center of learning, attracting scholars and students from far and wide.

Krakow's history took a dark turn during World War II when it fell under Nazi occupation. The Jewish population, which had thrived in the Kazimierz district, was subjected to persecution and ultimately faced the horrors of the Holocaust. The nearby Auschwitz-Birkenau concentration camp stands as a grim reminder of this tragic chapter in history.

After the war, Krakow became part of the communist People's Republic of Poland. The city underwent significant restoration and revitalization efforts, preserving its historical landmarks and reclaiming its cultural identity. In 1978, Krakow's historic center was designated as a UNESCO World Heritage site, acknowledging its outstanding universal value.

In more recent years, Krakow has emerged as a thriving tourist destination, attracting visitors from around the world. Its well-preserved medieval architecture, vibrant cultural scene, and warm hospitality make it an enchanting city to explore.

Today, Krakow stands as a testament to resilience and the enduring spirit of its people. It offers a unique blend of history, art, and traditions, creating a captivating atmosphere that captivates both locals and tourists alike. Krakow's brief history is a tapestry woven with triumphs and tragedies, shaping the city into the captivating destination it is today.

Krakow's Weather

Krakow, located in southern Poland, experiences a temperate continental climate characterized by distinct seasons. The city's weather is influenced by its inland location, the proximity of the Carpathian Mountains, and the presence of the Vistula River.

Spring (March to May) in Krakow is generally mild with fluctuating temperatures. March can still feel quite chilly, with occasional frost and snow, while April and May see gradual warming. During spring, the city begins to bloom, and the parks and gardens come alive with colorful flowers and foliage.

Summer (June to August) in Krakow is pleasantly warm, with temperatures averaging between 20 to 25 degrees Celsius (68 to 77 degrees Fahrenheit). It is the peak tourist season, with long daylight hours and a lively atmosphere. However, occasional heatwaves can push temperatures higher, reaching the 30-degree Celsius (86-degree Fahrenheit) mark. Summer is a great time to explore outdoor attractions, enjoy outdoor cafes, and experience various festivals and events.

Autumn (September to November) in Krakow brings cooler temperatures and a tapestry of vibrant fall colors. September is usually mild and pleasant, while October and November witness a gradual transition into winter. It is advisable to have layered clothing during this season as the temperatures can vary significantly throughout the day.

Winter (December to February) in Krakow is cold, with temperatures often dropping below freezing. Snowfall is common, creating a picturesque winter wonderland. December is the beginning of the winter season, and the city is adorned with festive decorations and Christmas markets. January and February are the coldest months, with temperatures often ranging from -5 to -10 degrees Celsius (23 to 14 degrees Fahrenheit). It is important to dress warmly and be prepared for the possibility of icy conditions.

Krakow's weather can be changeable, and it is always wise to check the forecast before planning outdoor activities. The city experiences a moderate level of rainfall throughout the year, with slightly higher precipitation in the summer months.

Overall, Krakow offers a diverse climate that showcases the beauty of each season. Whether it's the blossoming of spring, the warmth of summer, the colors of autumn, or the enchantment of winter, the city's weather adds to its charm and provides a unique experience for visitors throughout the year.

Best Time to Visit Krakow

The best time to visit Krakow largely depends on personal preferences and the type of experience one seeks. Each season in Krakow has its own unique charm and attractions to offer, so choosing the ideal time to visit requires considering various factors.

The summer months of June, July, and August are the peak tourist season in Krakow. The weather is generally warm and pleasant, with temperatures ranging from 20 to 25 degrees Celsius (68 to 77 degrees Fahrenheit). This period is perfect for exploring outdoor attractions, enjoying the lively atmosphere, and attending various festivals and events. However, it is worth noting that popular tourist sites can be crowded, and accommodation prices may be higher during this time. It is advisable to book accommodations and attractions in advance to ensure availability.

For those seeking milder temperatures and fewer crowds, spring and autumn are great times to visit. Spring (March to May) brings mild weather, blossoming flowers, and a refreshing atmosphere. The parks and gardens are particularly enchanting during this time. Autumn (September to November) offers pleasant temperatures, stunning fall foliage, and a quieter ambiance. These shoulder seasons provide a more relaxed and immersive experience, allowing visitors to enjoy the city's attractions at a leisurely pace.

Winter in Krakow (December to February) can be quite cold, with temperatures often dropping below freezing. However, this season has its own appeal, especially during the festive period leading up to Christmas. The city is adorned with decorations, and Christmas markets create a magical atmosphere. Winter is also an excellent time to experience traditional Polish cuisine, warm up with a cup of hot mulled wine, and enjoy the beauty of snow-covered landscapes.

Ultimately, the best time to visit Krakow depends on individual preferences. Whether it's the bustling energy of summer, the vibrant colors of spring and autumn, or the enchantment of winter, Krakow offers something unique throughout the year. It is advisable to consider factors such as weather, crowd levels, and personal interests when planning a visit to ensure a memorable and enjoyable experience.

How To Get There

Getting to Krakow is relatively easy, thanks to its well-connected transportation network. Whether traveling by air, train, or bus, there are several options available to reach this charming Polish city.

By Air:

Krakow has an international airport called Krakow John Paul II International Airport (KRK), located about 11 kilometers west of the city center. The airport serves numerous domestic and international flights, making it a convenient option for travelers from around the world. From the airport, visitors can reach the city center by taxi, shuttle bus, or public transportation.

By Train:

Krakow has excellent rail connections, making it easily accessible from other Polish cities and European destinations. The city's main train station, Krakow Glowny, is centrally located and serves as a major transportation hub. High-speed trains, regional trains, and international connections are available, allowing for a flexible and convenient travel experience. Travelers can check train schedules and book tickets in advance to secure their preferred departure times.

By Bus:

Bus travel is another popular option for reaching Krakow. The city is well-served by domestic and international bus connections, offering a cost-effective means of transportation. The main bus station, Krakow MDA, is conveniently located near the city center and is easily accessible by public transportation. Various bus companies operate services to and from Krakow, providing a wide range of routes and departure times.

By Car:

For those who prefer the flexibility and independence of driving, reaching Krakow by car is also an option. The city is well-connected to Poland's major road networks, making it accessible from various directions. However, it is important to note that traffic and parking can be challenging in the city center, especially during peak tourist seasons. It is advisable to research parking options in advance or consider using public transportation once in the city.

Once in Krakow, getting around the city is relatively easy. The public transportation system includes trams and buses, offering convenient options for navigating the city and reaching various attractions. Taxis are also readily available, but it is recommended to use licensed and reputable taxi companies.

Top 15 Reasons To Plan A Trip To Krakow As Your Next Vacation Destination

Krakow, the historic city in southern Poland, offers a plethora of reasons why it should be your next vacation destination. Here are the top 15 reasons to plan a trip to Krakow:

1. **Rich History**: Explore the city's fascinating history, from its medieval roots to its significance during World War II and the Holocaust.
2. **Wawel Castle:** Visit the iconic Wawel Castle, a symbol of Polish royalty and a treasure trove of art, history, and stunning architecture.
3. **Old Town Charm**: Wander through the enchanting streets of the UNESCO-listed Old

Town, lined with colorful buildings, charming cafés, and bustling market squares.

4. **St. Mary's Basilica:** Admire the majestic St. Mary's Basilica, known for its exquisite Gothic architecture and the famous hourly trumpet call from its tower.

5. **Jewish Heritage:** Explore the historic Jewish Quarter, Kazimierz, with its synagogues, museums, and vibrant cultural scene.

6. **Auschwitz-Birkenau:** Pay tribute to the victims of the Holocaust by visiting the nearby Auschwitz-Birkenau concentration camp, a powerful and somber experience.

7. **Underground Wonders:** Discover the secrets of Krakow's Underground Museum, showcasing the city's archaeological treasures and its hidden underground world.

8. **Jagiellonian University:** Marvel at the prestigious Jagiellonian University, one of Europe's oldest universities, and visit its historic Collegium Maius.

9. **Cultural Festivals:** Experience Krakow's vibrant cultural scene by attending one of its many festivals, including the famous Krakow Film Festival and the International Cultural Heritage Festival.

10. **Traditional Cuisine:** Indulge in delicious Polish cuisine, including pierogies, Polish sausages,

hearty soups, and delectable pastries like the famous paczki.

11. **Vistula River:** Take a relaxing stroll along the banks of the picturesque Vistula River, offering beautiful views and a serene escape from the bustling city center.

12. **Museums and Art Galleries:** Immerse yourself in art and culture at Krakow's renowned museums and galleries, such as the National Museum and the Museum of Contemporary Art in Krakow (MOCAK).

13. **Zakrzowek Quarry:** Visit the stunning Zakrzowek Quarry, a former limestone quarry turned crystal-clear lake, perfect for swimming, diving, and enjoying nature.

14. **Vibrant Nightlife**: Experience Krakow's vibrant nightlife scene, with its array of bars, clubs, and live music venues that cater to every taste and preference.

15. **Warm Hospitality:** Discover the warm and welcoming nature of the Polish people, known for their hospitality and eagerness to share their culture and history with visitors.

With its rich history, captivating architecture, vibrant cultural scene, and warm hospitality, Krakow offers an unforgettable vacation experience. Whether you are interested in history, art, food, or simply immersing yourself in the charm of a European city, Krakow is sure to leave a lasting impression and create memories that will stay with you long after your trip.

CHAPTER 2: TIPS AND CONSIDERATIONS

Visiting Krakow On A Budget

Visiting Krakow on a budget is entirely feasible, as the city offers numerous affordable options for accommodations, dining, and attractions. Here are some tips on how to make the most of your budget while exploring this captivating Polish city.

Accommodations: Krakow offers a range of budget-friendly accommodations, including hostels, guesthouses, and budget hotels. Staying in the city center or in the nearby Kazimierz district provides easy access to major attractions and saves transportation costs.

Transportation: Krakow has an efficient public transportation system, including trams and buses, which are affordable and convenient for getting around the city. Consider purchasing a multi-day public transportation pass to save on individual fares.

Free Attractions: Krakow has several free attractions, allowing you to explore the city without breaking the bank. These include wandering through the charming streets of the Old Town, visiting the grounds of Wawel Castle, and admiring the exterior of St. Mary's Basilica. You can also explore the city's parks, such as Planty Park or the picturesque Jordan Park.

Discounted Tickets: Many attractions in Krakow offer discounted or reduced-price tickets for students, seniors, or specific time slots. Take advantage of these offers to visit museums, art galleries, and historical sites at a lower cost.

Street Food and Local Eateries: Krakow is known for its delicious street food and affordable local eateries. Try traditional Polish snacks like zapiekanki (toasted baguette with toppings) or visit milk bars for budget-friendly meals that showcase authentic Polish cuisine.

Market Hall: Visit the Krakow Market Hall (Hala Targowa) to find fresh produce, local products, and inexpensive food options. It's a great place to grab a quick and affordable meal.

Free Walking Tours: Joining a free walking tour is an excellent way to explore Krakow while learning about its history and culture. Many tour companies offer free tours, allowing you to experience the city's highlights without spending a fortune.

By following these tips, you can enjoy a budget-friendly visit to Krakow without sacrificing the opportunity to explore its historical sites, sample its cuisine, and immerse yourself in its vibrant atmosphere. Remember, it's the experiences and memories that matter most, and Krakow offers plenty of those regardless of your budget.

Getting Around Krakow

Kraków is a relatively small city, so it is easy to get around on foot or by public transportation. The Old Town and Kazimierz are both compact and pedestrian-friendly, and most of the major attractions are within walking distance of each other. If you want to explore further afield, there are trams and buses that run throughout the city.

1. **Public transportation** is the cheapest way to get around Kraków. A single ticket for a 20-minute journey costs 2.80 zloty (about $0.60), and a single ticket for an hour costs 5 zloty (about $1). You can also buy day passes, 3-day passes, and weekly passes.
2. **Taxis** are another option, but they can be more expensive than public transportation. The base fare for a taxi in Kraków is 6 zloty (about $1.50),

and the fare increases by 2.40 zloty (about $0.50) per kilometer.

3. **Bicycles** are a great way to get around Kraków if you're fit and active. There are several bike-sharing companies in the city, and you can rent a bike for as little as 5 zloty (about $1) per hour.

4. **Walking** is the cheapest and most environmentally friendly way to get around Kraków. The Old Town and Kazimierz are both compact and pedestrian-friendly, and most of the major attractions are within walking distance of each other.

Shopping In Krakow

Krakow is a great city for shopping. There are a wide variety of stores to choose from, including high-end designer brands, local boutiques, and souvenir shops. You can find everything from clothes and shoes to souvenirs and electronics.

Here are some of the best places to shop in Krakow:

1. Galeria Krakowska is the largest shopping mall in Krakow. It has over 250 stores, including Zara, H&M, and Sephora.
2. Vitkac is a luxury shopping mall located in the Old Town. It has a wide selection of designer brands, such as Gucci, Prada, and Louis Vuitton.
3. Kazimierz is a historic district that is now home to a number of trendy boutiques and art galleries. This is a great place to find unique souvenirs and gifts.
4. Smocza Jama is a flea market located in the Old Town. It's a great place to find hidden treasures, such as antiques, vintage clothes, and second-hand books.

Estimated expenses for shopping in Krakow:

- T-shirt: 20-30 PLN ($5-7)
- Pair of jeans: 50-100 PLN ($12-25)
- Pair of shoes: 100-200 PLN ($25-50)
- Souvenir: 10-20 PLN ($2.50-5)
- Dinner for two at a mid-range restaurant: 100-150 PLN ($25-37.50)

5 Inexpensive Krakow Hotel Option

1. Krakow B&B - Bed & Breakfast. This hotel is located in the Old Town and offers simple, but comfortable rooms with free Wi-Fi and breakfast. It is about a 10-minute walk from the Wawel Castle and the Main Market Square. Estimated expenses:

- Double room: 100-150 PLN ($25-37.50) per night
- Breakfast: 20 PLN ($5) per person

2. Hotel Pollera. This hotel is located in the Old Town and offers spacious rooms with free Wi-Fi and breakfast. It is about a 5-minute walk from the Wawel Castle and the Main Market Square. Estimated expenses:

- Double room: 150-200 PLN ($37.50-50) per night
- Breakfast: 25 PLN ($6.25) per person

3. ibis budget Krakow Stare Miasto. This hotel is located in the Old Town and offers modern rooms with free Wi-Fi and breakfast. It is about a 15-minute walk from the Wawel Castle and the Main Market Square. Estimated expenses:

- Double room: 100-150 PLN ($25-37.50) per night
- Breakfast: 15 PLN ($3.75) per person

4. Osada Hostel. This hostel is located in the Kazimierz district and offers dormitory rooms and

private rooms with shared bathrooms. It is about a 10-minute walk from the Old Town. Estimated expenses:

- Dorm bed: 30-40 PLN ($7.50-10) per night
- Private room: 70-100 PLN ($17.50-25) per night

5. Hostel4u Krakow. This hostel is located in the Podgórze district and offers dormitory rooms and private rooms with shared bathrooms. It is about a 20-minute walk from the Old Town. Estimated expenses:

- Dorm bed: 30-40 PLN ($7.50-10) per night
- Private room: 60-80 PLN ($15-20) per night

5 Luxurious Places To Stay In Krakow

1. Hotel Unicus Palace. This 5-star hotel is located in the Old Town and offers spacious rooms with stunning views of the city. It has a spa, an indoor pool, and a rooftop terrace. Estimated expenses:
*   Double room: 500-700 PLN ($125-175) per night
*   Breakfast: 35 PLN ($8.75) per person

2. H15 Palace Hotel. This 5-star hotel is located in the Old Town and offers elegant rooms with

modern amenities. It has a spa, a restaurant, and a bar. Estimated expenses:

- Double room: 600-800 PLN ($150-200) per night
- Breakfast: 40 PLN ($10) per person

3. Balthasar Design Hotel. This 5-star hotel is located in the Kazimierz district and offers stylish rooms with a touch of Art Deco. It has a restaurant, a bar, and a rooftop terrace with views of the city. Estimated expenses:

- Double room: 400-600 PLN ($100-150) per night
- Breakfast: 30 PLN ($7.50) per person

4. ARThotel by Vienna House. This 5-star hotel is located in the Old Town and offers contemporary rooms with floor-to-ceiling windows. It has a spa, a restaurant, and a bar. Estimated expenses:

- Double room: 500-700 PLN ($125-175) per night
- Breakfast: 35 PLN ($8.75) per person

5. Hotel Puro Krakow Stare Miasto. This 4-star hotel is located in the Old Town and offers modern rooms with minimalist decor. It has a restaurant, a bar, and a rooftop terrace with views of the city.

Estimated expenses:
- Double room: 400-600 PLN ($100-150) per night
- Breakfast: 30 PLN ($7.50) per person

CHAPTER 3

Top 5 Event In Krakow

1. Wianki (The Luminous Night of the John's Night) - Held annually in June, Wianki is a popular summer solstice celebration in Krakow. The event takes place along the banks of the Vistula River and features music concerts, performances, and a spectacular fireworks display. Thousands of people gather to release lit paper lanterns into the night sky, creating a magical and unforgettable atmosphere.

2. Krakow Christmas Market - During the holiday season, Krakow transforms into a winter wonderland with its charming Christmas market. Located in the Main Market Square, the market

offers a festive ambiance with beautifully decorated stalls selling traditional Polish crafts, Christmas decorations, and delicious food. Visitors can enjoy mulled wine, roasted chestnuts, and various treats while soaking in the enchanting atmosphere.

3. Krakow Film Festival - As one of the oldest and most prestigious film festivals in Europe, the Krakow Film Festival attracts filmmakers, industry professionals, and movie enthusiasts from around the world. Held annually in May or June, the festival showcases a wide range of documentary, short, and animated films. It is a fantastic opportunity to discover innovative and thought-provoking cinema.

4. Pierogi Festival - Pierogi, the iconic Polish dumplings, take center stage during the Pierogi Festival in August. The festival celebrates this beloved Polish dish with various vendors offering a vast array of pierogi fillings and flavors. From traditional favorites to unique combinations, visitors can savor different types of pierogi while enjoying live music, cultural performances, and other activities.

5. Festival of Polish Music - Dedicated to promoting Polish classical music, the Festival of Polish Music takes place in September and October. Renowned musicians and orchestras come together to perform works by Polish composers, showcasing the country's rich musical heritage. The festival includes concerts, recitals, and educational events, providing a captivating experience for music lovers.

3 Days Krakow Travel Plan

Day 1:

Morning:
- Arrive in Krakow and check into your accommodation.

- Start your day with a visit to the historic Wawel Castle and explore its beautiful grounds and exhibits. Entry fee: 30 PLN (approx. $8).

Afternoon:

- Head to the Main Market Square and visit St. Mary's Basilica. Entry fee: 10 PLN (approx. $3).
- Enjoy a traditional Polish lunch at a local eatery. Budget: 40 PLN (approx. $11).

Evening:

- Take a relaxing stroll along the Vistula River and enjoy the picturesque views.
- Have dinner at a local restaurant in the Kazimierz district. Budget: 50 PLN (approx. $14).
- Day 1 expenses estimate: 130 PLN (approx. $36).

Day 2:

Morning:
- Start the day with a visit to the Auschwitz-Birkenau Memorial and Museum. Take a guided tour for a deeper understanding of the historical significance. Transportation and tour fee: 100 PLN (approx. $28).

Afternoon:

- Return to Krakow and have lunch at a local café or restaurant. Budget: 40 PLN (approx. $11).
- Visit the Krakow Underground Museum and explore its archaeological treasures. Entry fee: 25 PLN (approx. $7).

Evening:

- Experience Krakow's vibrant nightlife in the Main Market Square. Enjoy drinks and live music at one of the local bars. Budget: 80 PLN (approx. $22).
- Day 2 expenses estimate: 245 PLN (approx. $68).

Day 3:

Morning:
- Explore the Kazimierz district, known for its rich Jewish heritage. Visit the historic synagogues and the Galicia Jewish Museum. Entry fees: 20 PLN (approx. $6).
- Grab a quick and affordable lunch from a local street food vendor. Budget: 20 PLN (approx. $6).

Afternoon:
- Discover the artistic side of Krakow at the Museum of Contemporary Art in Krakow (MOCAK). Entry fee: 14 PLN (approx. $4).

- Take a leisurely stroll through Planty Park, a beautiful green space surrounding the Old Town.

Evening:
- Enjoy a farewell dinner at a traditional Polish restaurant. Budget: 60 PLN (approx. $17).
- Day 3 expenses estimate: 114 PLN (approx. $32).
- Total estimated expenses for 3 days: 489 PLN (approx. $136).

7 Days Krakow Travel Plan

Day 1:

Morning:
- Arrive in Krakow and check into your accommodation.
- Explore the historic Wawel Castle and its grounds. Entry fee: 30 PLN (approx. $8).

Afternoon:

- Visit St. Mary's Basilica in the Main Market Square. Entry fee: 10 PLN (approx. $3).
- Enjoy a traditional Polish lunch at a local restaurant. Budget: 40 PLN (approx. $11).

Evening:

- Take a relaxing walk along the Vistula River and enjoy the scenic views.
- Have dinner at a restaurant in the Kazimierz district. Budget: 50 PLN (approx. $14).
- Day 1 expenses estimate: 130 PLN (approx. $36).

Day 2:

Morning:

- Take a day trip to the Auschwitz-Birkenau Memorial and Museum. Join a guided tour for a comprehensive experience. Transportation and tour fee: 100 PLN (approx. $28).

Afternoon:

- Return to Krakow and have lunch at a local eatery. Budget: 40 PLN (approx. $11).
- Explore the Krakow Underground Museum. Entry fee: 25 PLN (approx. $7).

Evening:

- Experience the vibrant nightlife of the Main Market Square. Enjoy drinks and live music at one of the bars. Budget: 80 PLN (approx. $22).
- Day 2 expenses estimate: 245 PLN (approx. $68).

Day 3:

Morning:

- Visit the Oskar Schindler's Enamel Factory Museum. Entry fee: 24 PLN (approx. $7).

Afternoon:

- Explore the historic Jewish Quarter, Kazimierz,

and visit its synagogues and museums.
- Have lunch at a local restaurant. Budget: 40 PLN (approx. $11).

Evening:
- Enjoy a performance at the Juliusz Słowacki Theatre or the Krakow Philharmonic. Ticket prices vary.
- Day 3 expenses estimate: 64 PLN+ (approx. $18+).

Day 4:

Morning:
- Take a day trip to the Wieliczka Salt Mine. Join a guided tour to explore the fascinating underground chambers. Transportation and tour fee: 100 PLN (approx. $28).

Afternoon:
- Return to Krakow and have lunch at a local eatery.

Budget: 40 PLN (approx. $11).
- Explore the Museum of Contemporary Art in Krakow (MOCAK). Entry fee: 14 PLN (approx. $4).

Evening:
- Enjoy dinner at a traditional Polish restaurant. Budget: 60 PLN (approx. $17).
- Day 4 expenses estimate: 214 PLN (approx. $60).

Day 5:

Morning:
- Visit the Schindler's List filming locations and walk through the former Jewish Ghetto.
- Have lunch at a local café or restaurant. Budget: 40 PLN (approx. $11).

Afternoon:
- Take a relaxing boat ride on the Vistula River.
- Visit the Manggha Museum of Japanese Art and

Technology. Entry fee: 15 PLN (approx. $4).

Evening:
- Explore the Planty Park and enjoy a picnic or a leisurely walk.
- Day 5 expenses estimate: 55 PLN (approx. $15).

Day 6:

Morning:
- Explore the Kosciuszko Mound, offering panoramic views of the city. Entry fee: 14 PLN (approx. $4).

Afternoon:
- Visit the Czartoryski Museum, home to Leonardo da Vinci's famous painting, "Lady with an Ermine." Entry fee: 25 PLN (approx. $7).
- Have lunch at a local eatery. Budget: 40 PLN (approx. $11).
- Explore the beautiful Botanic Garden of the

Jagiellonian University. Entry fee: 15 PLN (approx. $4).

Evening:

- Enjoy a leisurely walk along the Royal Route, taking in the historic landmarks and charming atmosphere.
- Indulge in a delicious dinner at a restaurant of your choice. Budget: 60 PLN (approx. $17).
- Day 6 expenses estimate: 154 PLN (approx. $43).

Day 7:

Morning:

- Take a day trip to the stunning Tatra Mountains and visit the Zakopane resort town. Transportation costs vary depending on the chosen method.

Afternoon:

- Explore the charming streets of Zakopane, admire the traditional wooden architecture, and enjoy the beautiful mountain scenery.
- Have lunch at a local restaurant. Budget: 50 PLN (approx. $14).

Evening:

- Return to Krakow and spend your final evening enjoying the vibrant nightlife or simply relaxing and reflecting on your trip.
- Have a farewell dinner at a restaurant of your choice. Budget: 60 PLN (approx. $17).
- Day 7 expenses estimate: Variable depending on the chosen day trip.
- Total estimated expenses for 7 days: Approx. 988 PLN+ (approx. $275+).

CHAPTER 4: PLANNING A TRIP TO KRAKOW

What To Take For Your Trip

When packing for your trip to Krakow, it's essential to consider the season, weather conditions, and the activities you plan to engage in. Here are some essential items to take with you to ensure a comfortable and enjoyable stay in this captivating Polish city.

1. Clothing: The weather in Krakow can vary depending on the season, so it's important to pack accordingly. For the summer months (June to August), pack lightweight and breathable clothing such as t-shirts, shorts, dresses, and skirts. Don't

forget to bring a light jacket or sweater for cooler evenings. In the spring and autumn (April to May and September to October), pack layers including long-sleeved shirts, sweaters, and a light jacket or coat. For the winter months (November to March), pack warm clothing including thermal layers, sweaters, a heavy coat, hats, scarves, and gloves.

2. Comfortable Shoes: Krakow is a city best explored on foot, so comfortable walking shoes are a must. Pack a pair of sturdy walking shoes or sneakers that can withstand long hours of exploration on cobblestone streets.

3. Travel Adapters: The power outlets in Poland use the Europlug (Type C) or Schuko plug (Type E/F). Depending on your home country, you may need a travel adapter to charge your electronic devices.

4. Medications and First Aid Kit: If you take any prescription medications, be sure to pack an ample supply for the duration of your trip. It's also advisable to bring a basic first aid kit that includes items like band-aids, pain relievers, antihistamines, and any other personal medications you may require.

5. Travel Documents: Remember to bring your passport, visa (if required), travel insurance information, and any other necessary travel documents. It's a good idea to make copies of these

documents and keep them separate from the originals.

6. Local Currency: The official currency in Poland is the Polish złoty (PLN). While credit cards are widely accepted, it's always useful to have some local currency on hand for small purchases or places that may not accept cards.

7. Guidebooks and Maps: Consider bringing a guidebook or downloading a travel app to help navigate the city and learn more about its attractions, history, and culture. Additionally, having a physical map or using a navigation app on your phone can be helpful for exploring the city streets.

8. Miscellaneous Items: Other items to consider packing include a reusable water bottle, sunscreen, sunglasses, an umbrella or raincoat (depending on the season), a daypack for carrying essentials during sightseeing, and a camera to capture the beautiful moments.

Remember to pack according to your personal needs and preferences, and be mindful of any specific activities or events you plan to participate in during your stay in Krakow. By packing smartly, you can ensure a stress-free and enjoyable trip to this enchanting city.

Night Spot In Krakow

Krakow, a city renowned for its vibrant nightlife, offers a wide array of night spots that cater to all tastes and preferences. Whether you're seeking trendy bars, bustling clubs, or cozy pubs, Krakow has something for everyone. Here are some popular nightspots in Krakow that you shouldn't miss:

1. Main Market Square (Rynek Główny): The heart of Krakow's nightlife, the Main Market Square comes alive at night. With its picturesque surroundings and numerous bars and restaurants, it offers a lively atmosphere for socializing and enjoying a night out with friends. You can grab a drink, listen to live music, or simply soak in the charming ambiance of this historic square.

2. Kazimierz District: Known as the city's bohemian quarter, Kazimierz is a hub for nightlife in Krakow. Its narrow streets are lined with an eclectic mix of bars, pubs, and clubs. Here, you can find everything from trendy cocktail bars and craft beer pubs to underground clubs playing a variety of music genres. Kazimierz is also home to numerous cultural events, including live performances, art exhibitions, and film screenings.

3. Plac Nowy: Located in the heart of the Jewish Quarter, Plac Nowy is a bustling square that transforms into a lively nightlife hotspot after dark. The square is known for its iconic rotunda, housing the famous Zapiekanka stalls where you can grab a late-night snack. Surrounding the square, you'll find a range of bars and clubs, each with its own unique vibe and atmosphere.

4. Beer Gardens: Krakow is known for its beer culture, and beer gardens are popular gathering spots for locals and tourists alike. These outdoor venues offer a relaxed and social atmosphere, perfect for enjoying a refreshing drink on warm summer evenings. Many beer gardens serve a variety of local and international brews, and some even offer live music or outdoor screenings of sporting events.

5. Jazz Clubs: Krakow has a rich jazz scene, with several clubs dedicated to this genre of music. Jazz

lovers can enjoy live performances by local and international artists in intimate settings. The ambiance is cozy and inviting, providing the perfect backdrop for an evening of soulful tunes and smooth melodies.

6. Student Bars: As a university city, Krakow is filled with student-friendly bars that offer affordable drinks and a lively atmosphere. These bars cater to a younger crowd and often feature themed nights, live music, and DJs spinning popular tunes. It's a great way to mingle with locals, meet fellow travelers, and experience the energetic spirit of Krakow's nightlife.

Culture And People

The culture and people of Krakow are deeply rooted in history, traditions, and a strong sense of community. As one of Poland's oldest and most culturally significant cities, Krakow is known for its rich heritage, architectural wonders, and vibrant arts scene. Here are some key aspects of Krakow's culture and the characteristics of its people:

1. Historical Significance: Krakow's historical significance is evident in its well-preserved medieval architecture, including the iconic Wawel Castle and St. Mary's Basilica. The city was once the capital of Poland and served as the center of political, economic, and cultural life for centuries. Its past has left an indelible mark on the city's identity and serves as a source of pride for its residents.

2. Art and Literature: Krakow is a hub of artistic expression, attracting artists, writers, and musicians from all over the world. The city hosts numerous festivals, exhibitions, and cultural events throughout the year, such as the Krakow Film Festival and the Krakow Photomonth. It is also home to prestigious art schools and galleries that showcase a wide range of artistic styles and genres.
3. Intellectual Legacy: Krakow has a long-standing intellectual legacy, with its prestigious Jagiellonian University being one of the oldest universities in the world. The university has nurtured great minds and produced renowned scholars, scientists, and thinkers who have made significant contributions to various fields of study.
4. Warm Hospitality: The people of Krakow are known for their warm hospitality and welcoming nature. They take pride in their city and are often eager to share its history, traditions, and hidden gems with visitors. Krakow's residents are friendly, approachable, and enthusiastic about their local culture, making it easy for travelers to engage with them and learn more about the city's traditions.
5. Traditional Festivities: Krakow celebrates its cultural heritage through traditional festivities and events. One of the most significant is the annual Krakow Christmas Market, where locals and tourists gather to enjoy festive decorations, local cuisine, and traditional crafts. The city also hosts vibrant music festivals, including the Krakow

Jewish Culture Festival and the Sacrum Profanum Festival, which showcase a diverse range of artistic performances.

6. Love for Food and Drink: Krakow's culinary scene is a reflection of its cultural diversity. The city boasts numerous traditional Polish restaurants serving delicious dishes like pierogi (dumplings), żurek (sour rye soup), and oscypek (smoked sheep cheese). Krakow is also home to a thriving café culture, where locals gather to enjoy a cup of coffee and indulge in delectable pastries.

The culture and people of Krakow embody a strong sense of pride in their history, a passion for the arts, and a warm and welcoming attitude towards visitors. Exploring the city's cultural treasures and interacting with its people provides a unique and enriching experience, allowing travelers to immerse themselves in the heart and soul of this captivating Polish city.

CHAPTER 5

Top 10 Best Local Cuisine In Krakow

When visiting Krakow, you'll be delighted by the diverse and mouthwatering local cuisine. From traditional Polish dishes to international influences, here is a list of the top 10 best local cuisines you must try in Krakow:

1. Pierogi: These delicious dumplings are a Polish classic. They come in various fillings, such as potato and cheese, meat, mushroom, or fruit. Served boiled, fried, or baked, pierogi are a must-try dish.

2. Bigos: Also known as "hunter's stew," bigos is a hearty dish made with sauerkraut, fresh cabbage, various meats (typically pork, beef, and sausage),

and aromatic spices. It's a true comfort food and a favorite during colder months.

3. Zurek: This traditional sour rye soup is a popular Polish dish. It features a tangy broth made from fermented rye flour and is typically served with boiled potatoes, sausage, and hard-boiled eggs.

4. Oscypek: Hailing from the nearby Tatra Mountains, oscypek is a distinctively shaped smoked sheep cheese. It's often grilled and served with cranberry sauce, making for a delightful and savory snack.

5. Placki ziemniaczane: These crispy potato pancakes are a staple in Polish cuisine. Served with sour cream or applesauce, they make a delicious appetizer or side dish.

6. Barszcz: A vibrant beetroot soup, barszcz is a classic Polish dish known for its bright red color. It can be enjoyed hot or cold and is often served with a dollop of sour cream.

7. Kielbasa: Polish sausage, or kielbasa, comes in a variety of types and flavors. Whether grilled, boiled, or pan-fried, it's a delicious and satisfying dish that pairs well with mustard and sauerkraut.

8. Makowiec: This poppy seed roll is a traditional Polish dessert that is enjoyed during special occasions and holidays. The roll is filled with a sweet and nutty poppy seed mixture and often dusted with powdered sugar.

9. Sernik: Polish cheesecake, or sernik, is a creamy and dense dessert made with farmer's cheese or quark. It has a delicate flavor and can be served plain or with various toppings, such as fruit compote or chocolate sauce.

10. Obwarzanek: Similar to a bagel, obwarzanek is a ring-shaped bread sprinkled with salt, poppy seeds, sesame seeds, or cheese. It's a popular street food in Krakow and makes for a tasty and satisfying snack.

Money Matters And Saving Tips

When traveling to Krakow, it's important to have a good understanding of money matters and implement some saving tips to make the most of your budget. Here are some key considerations and tips to help you manage your finances while exploring this beautiful city:

1. Currency: The official currency in Krakow is the Polish złoty (PLN). It's advisable to exchange your currency for złoty upon arrival or withdraw cash from ATMs, which are widely available throughout the city. Be mindful of exchange rates and fees to ensure you get the best value for your money.

2. Credit Cards: Major credit cards are widely accepted in Krakow, especially in hotels, restaurants, and larger establishments. However, it's always a good idea to carry some cash for smaller vendors, local markets, and public transportation.

3. Budgeting: Plan your daily expenses in advance to avoid overspending. Allocate a budget for accommodation, meals, transportation, sightseeing, and shopping, and try to stick to it. Consider using budgeting apps or keeping a record of your expenses to stay on track.

4. Eating Out: Krakow offers a range of dining options to suit various budgets. To save money on meals, consider eating at local eateries, street food

stalls, or "milk bars" (budget-friendly self-service cafeterias). These establishments offer delicious and affordable Polish cuisine.

5. Free and Low-Cost Activities: Take advantage of the many free or low-cost attractions in Krakow. Explore the charming Old Town, visit the numerous churches and synagogues, or relax in the city's beautiful parks. Many museums and cultural institutions offer discounted or free admission on certain days or during specific hours.

6. Public Transportation: Krakow has a well-developed public transportation system, including buses and trams, which is a cost-effective way to get around the city. Consider purchasing a transportation pass or ticket bundles for multiple journeys to save money.

7. Souvenir Shopping: Look for authentic and locally made souvenirs at markets and smaller shops, where you may find unique items at more affordable prices compared to touristy areas. Remember to bargain if appropriate.

8. Water: Instead of buying bottled water, refill a reusable water bottle at fountains or use tap water, which is safe to drink in Krakow.

9. Timing: Consider visiting Krakow during the shoulder seasons (spring and autumn) when accommodation and flight prices may be more affordable compared to peak tourist seasons.

10. Discounts and City Cards: Check for discounted tickets, passes, or city cards that offer savings on attractions, transportation, and restaurants. The Krakow Tourist Card, for example, provides free entry to many museums, discounts, and unlimited public transportation.

Local Customs And Etiquette

When visiting Krakow, it's important to be aware of the local customs and etiquette to show respect for the city's culture and its people. Here are some key customs and etiquette tips to keep in mind while in Krakow:

1. Greetings: When meeting someone for the first time, it is customary to offer a firm handshake and maintain eye contact. A polite greeting such as

"Dzień dobry" (Good day) or "Cześć" (Hello) is appropriate.

2. Politeness: Poles appreciate polite behavior. It's common to say "proszę" (please) and "dziękuję" (thank you) when making requests or receiving assistance. Showing gratitude is highly valued.

3. Table Manners: When dining, it is polite to wait until everyone is seated and the host begins eating before starting your meal. Keep your hands visible on the table but avoid resting your elbows. Finish all the food on your plate as leaving food may be considered wasteful.

4. Dress Code: Krakow has a relaxed dress code, but it's recommended to dress modestly and respectfully when visiting religious sites such as churches and synagogues. In some cases, you may be required to cover your shoulders and knees.

5. Public Behavior: Poles value personal space and expect others to respect it. Avoid loud and disruptive behavior in public places, including public transportation. Queue patiently and wait for your turn in lines.

6. Polite Address: When addressing someone, it is common to use formal titles such as "Pan" (Mr.) or "Pani" (Mrs./Ms.) followed by the person's last name. If the person is a friend or of a similar age, using their first name is acceptable.

7. Religious Sites: When visiting churches or synagogues, it is important to maintain a respectful and quiet demeanor. Dress modestly, and avoid talking loudly or taking photos unless it is permitted.

8. Smoking: Smoking is prohibited in most public places, including restaurants, bars, and public transportation. Be aware of designated smoking areas and follow the rules.

9. Photography: Always ask for permission before taking photos of people, especially in close-up shots. Some religious sites and museums may have restrictions on photography, so it's important to respect their rules

Tipping In Krakow

Tipping customs in Krakow, as in many parts of Poland, are generally appreciated but not mandatory. However, leaving a tip is a common practice to show appreciation for good service. Here are some guidelines for tipping in Krakow:

1. Restaurants: In restaurants, it is customary to leave a tip if you are satisfied with the service. A typical tip ranges from 10% to 15% of the total bill. You can either leave the cash directly on the table or inform the waiter that you would like to add a tip when paying by card.
2. Cafés and Bars: In cafés and bars, it's common to round up the bill or leave a small amount as a tip, especially if you received good service. For example, if your bill is 18 złoty, you can round it up to 20 złoty.
3. Taxis: It's customary to round up the fare to the nearest złoty or add a small tip, especially if the driver was helpful or provided a smooth ride. For example, if the fare is 25 złoty, you can round it up to 30 złoty.
4. Hotel Staff: If the hotel staff provides exceptional service, such as carrying your luggage or going above and beyond to assist you, you can leave a tip. You can give it directly to the staff member or leave it at the front desk in an envelope with their name on it.
5. Other Services: For other services like hair salons, spas, or tour guides, tipping is not obligatory but appreciated. You can leave a small tip, typically around 10% of the service cost, if you are satisfied

with the experience.

6. Service Charge: Some establishments may include a service charge (napiwek) in the bill, especially for larger groups or in touristy areas. In such cases, there is no obligation to leave an additional tip unless you want to show extra appreciation.

Remember that tipping is discretionary and based on your level of satisfaction with the service provided. If you have received exceptional service, a generous tip can be a way to express your gratitude. However, if you were dissatisfied, it is acceptable not to leave a tip or to leave a smaller amount. Ultimately, tipping in Krakow is a personal choice and should be done within your means and based on your own assessment of the service you received.

CHAPTER 6: TIPS AND CONSIDERATION ENTRY REQUIREMENT

Safety And Preparedness

Safety is an important aspect to consider when traveling to any destination, including Krakow. While Krakow is generally a safe city, it's always a good idea to take precautions and be prepared for any situation. Here are some tips to ensure your safety and preparedness during your visit to Krakow:

1. Stay Alert: Like in any tourist destination, be aware of your surroundings and stay alert, especially in crowded areas, public transportation,

and tourist attractions. Keep an eye on your belongings and avoid displaying expensive items or large amounts of cash.

2. Secure Your Belongings: Keep your valuables, including passports, money, and electronics, in a secure place such as a hotel safe. When you're out and about, carry a cross-body bag or backpack with secure zippers to deter pickpockets.

3. Emergency Numbers: Familiarize yourself with the local emergency contact numbers. In Poland, the general emergency number is 112 for police, ambulance, and fire emergencies. Additionally, make a note of your embassy's contact information in case of any major emergencies or assistance needs.

4. Transportation Safety: When using public transportation, be cautious of your belongings and avoid empty or poorly lit areas at night. Licensed taxis are generally safe, but it's advisable to use reputable taxi companies or order a taxi through a mobile app. Consider using ride-sharing services for added convenience and safety.

5. Be Cautious of Scams: Like in any tourist destination, be cautious of scams targeting tourists. Be wary of strangers offering unsolicited help or trying to distract you. Only use reputable tour operators and ticket vendors for attractions and events.

6. Drinking Responsibly: If you choose to consume alcohol, do so responsibly. Watch your drinks and avoid accepting drinks from strangers. It's also important to note that public drunkenness is not tolerated and can attract unwanted attention from both locals and law enforcement.

7. Emergency Preparedness: Familiarize yourself with the emergency exits and procedures at your accommodation. Keep a copy of your identification documents, travel insurance details, and important contact numbers in a safe place. Consider purchasing travel insurance to provide coverage for any unforeseen events or emergencies.

8. Health and Hygiene: Prioritize your health and hygiene by washing your hands regularly, especially before meals, and carrying hand sanitizer. If you require medication, ensure you have an adequate supply for the duration of your trip. If necessary, consult a healthcare professional before traveling.

9. Respect Local Customs and Laws: Familiarize yourself with the local customs and laws to ensure you behave respectfully and avoid any legal issues. For example, public drinking is prohibited in certain areas, and it's important to dress modestly when visiting religious sites.

10. Trust Your Instincts: Trust your instincts and if something feels unsafe or uncomfortable, remove yourself from the situation. It's always better to err on the side of caution and prioritize your personal safety.

11.

By being mindful of your surroundings, taking necessary precautions, and being prepared for any situation, you can ensure a safe and enjoyable visit to Krakow. Remember, your safety is paramount, so don't hesitate to seek assistance or report any concerns to the local authorities.

What To Do And What To Avoid When Visiting Krakow

When visiting Krakow, there are plenty of wonderful experiences to enjoy. However, it's also important to be mindful of certain things to do and avoid to ensure a smooth and enjoyable visit. Here are some tips on what to do and what to avoid when visiting Krakow:

What to Do:

- Explore the Old Town: Take time to wander through the charming streets of the Old Town, a UNESCO World Heritage site. Admire the stunning architecture, visit the Main Market Square, and explore the historic landmarks such as

St. Mary's Basilica and Wawel Castle.

- Visit Auschwitz-Birkenau: Pay a visit to Auschwitz-Birkenau, a significant historical site located near Krakow. This former Nazi concentration and extermination camp serves as a powerful memorial and a reminder of the atrocities of World War II.
- Discover the Jewish Quarter: Explore Kazimierz, the vibrant Jewish Quarter, known for its rich history and vibrant cultural scene. Visit synagogues, stroll through the bustling streets, and experience the unique blend of Jewish and Polish heritage.
- Enjoy Polish Cuisine: Indulge in the delicious local cuisine of Krakow. Try traditional dishes like pierogi (dumplings), żurek (sour rye soup), and oscypek (smoked sheep cheese). Visit local restaurants, milk bars, and food markets for an authentic culinary experience.
- Take a Day Trip to Wieliczka Salt Mine: Venture outside of Krakow and visit the Wieliczka Salt Mine, a remarkable underground complex with stunning salt-carved chambers, chapels, and saline lakes. It's an impressive site and a UNESCO World Heritage site.

What to Avoid:

- Disrespecting Religious Sites: When visiting churches or synagogues, dress modestly and behave respectfully. Avoid loud conversations, taking inappropriate photos, or any disrespectful behavior that could disturb others.

- Drinking in Public Places: Public drinking is prohibited in certain areas of Krakow. It's best to enjoy alcoholic beverages in licensed establishments such as bars, restaurants, or cafes rather than consuming them in public spaces.
- Unofficial Currency Exchanges: Be cautious when exchanging currency and avoid unofficial currency exchange booths or individuals offering currency exchange on the street. Stick to reputable exchange offices or withdraw money from ATMs.
- Engaging in Unlicensed Taxi Services: Be wary of unlicensed taxis to avoid scams or overcharging. Use official taxi stands or reputable taxi companies, or opt for ride-sharing services like Uber.
- Relying Solely on English: While many people in Krakow speak English, it's polite to learn a few basic Polish phrases and greetings. Attempting to communicate in Polish shows respect and can enhance your interactions with the locals.

CHAPTER 7: UNDERSTANDING INTERNATIONAL TRANSACTION FEES

Avoid Cell Phone Roaming Charges

Avoiding cell phone roaming charges while in Krakow can help you save money and stay connected without worrying about hefty bills. Here are some tips to help you avoid roaming charges:

1. Check with Your Service Provider: Before your trip, contact your cell phone service provider to inquire about international roaming plans or packages. They may have affordable options that allow you to use your phone abroad without incurring excessive charges. Consider activating a

temporary international plan that offers data, calling, and texting at a reasonable rate.

2. Use Wi-Fi: Take advantage of free Wi-Fi hotspots available in cafes, restaurants, hotels, and public areas in Krakow. Connect to these networks to access the internet, make voice and video calls, and use messaging apps without using your cellular data. Just ensure that the Wi-Fi network is secure and reliable before connecting.

3. Offline Maps and Navigation: Download offline maps of Krakow or use a navigation app that allows you to access maps and directions without an internet connection. This way, you can navigate the city without using your data plan.

4. Messaging Apps: Instead of sending traditional text messages, use messaging apps like WhatsApp, Viber, or Telegram that rely on internet connectivity. These apps allow you to send messages, make calls, and share media files over Wi-Fi or mobile data, thus avoiding SMS charges.

5. VoIP and Video Calling: Utilize voice over IP (VoIP) services such as Skype, FaceTime, or Google Hangouts to make international calls using an internet connection. These apps allow you to have audio or video calls with your loved ones without incurring high charges.

6. Purchase a Local SIM Card: If your phone is unlocked, you can purchase a local SIM card in Krakow. This option provides you with a local phone number and access to affordable local calling, texting, and data plans. Research and compare different providers to find the best option for your needs.

7. Data Roaming Settings: To avoid accidental data usage and charges, disable data roaming on your phone's settings. This way, your device won't automatically connect to mobile networks, ensuring that you solely rely on Wi-Fi for internet access.

8. Offline Usage of Apps: Many apps have offline capabilities, allowing you to use them without an internet connection. For example, you can download maps, travel guides, language translation apps, and entertainment content before your trip to use them offline while in Krakow.

Learn Basic Language

Learning some basic language skills can greatly enhance your experience in Krakow and make your interactions with locals more enjoyable. While many people in Krakow speak English, making an effort to learn a few basic Polish phrases can show respect and help you connect with the local culture. Here are some tips for learning basic language in Krakow:

1. Greetings: Start by learning basic greetings such as "Dzień dobry" (Good morning/afternoon), "Cześć" (Hello), and "Do widzenia" (Goodbye). These simple greetings can go a long way in creating a friendly atmosphere and showing your interest in the local language.

2. Polite Phrases: Learn phrases like "Proszę" (Please), "Dziękuję" (Thank you), and "Przepraszam" (Excuse me/I'm sorry). These polite expressions can help you navigate various situations, such as ordering food, asking for directions, or seeking assistance.

3. Numbers and Basic Vocabulary: Familiarize yourself with numbers, as they are essential for everyday interactions like shopping or asking for prices. Additionally, learn basic vocabulary related to food, transportation, and directions. Words like "Jedzenie" (Food), "Restauracja" (Restaurant), "Autobus" (Bus), "Pomoc" (Help), and "Gdzie jest...?" (Where is...?) can be particularly useful.

4. Language Apps and Online Resources: Take advantage of language learning apps and online resources to practice basic Polish phrases and vocabulary. Apps like Duolingo, Babbel, or

Memrise offer lessons and interactive exercises to help you learn at your own pace. You can also find online tutorials, phrasebooks, and language guides specific to Polish.

5. Language Exchange: Consider joining language exchange groups or finding language partners in Krakow. These groups provide an opportunity to practice conversational Polish with native speakers who are also interested in learning English or another language. It's a great way to improve your language skills while making new friends.

6. Cultural Immersion: Immerse yourself in the local culture by attending cultural events, visiting local markets, and exploring authentic Polish restaurants. Engaging with locals and practicing the language in real-life situations can enhance your learning experience and boost your confidence in speaking Polish.

7. Be Patient and Respectful: Remember that learning a new language takes time and practice. Be patient with yourself and others as you navigate conversations in Polish. Locals will appreciate your effort, even if your pronunciation or grammar isn't perfect. Polish is known for its challenging pronunciation, so don't be discouraged and keep practicing.

Learning even a few basic Polish phrases can make a positive impression and enhance your cultural experience in Krakow. The locals will appreciate your effort to connect with their language and culture. So, embrace the opportunity to learn, practice, and engage in conversations, and enjoy your time exploring Krakow with a newfound language skill.

Cash At The Airport Is Expensive

When traveling to Krakow, it's important to be aware that exchanging cash at the airport can be more expensive compared to other options in the city. Here's some information to keep in mind regarding cash exchange at the airport in Krakow:

1. Higher Exchange Rates: Exchange bureaus at airports often offer less favorable exchange rates

compared to those found in the city center or local banks. This means you may receive fewer Polish zlotys (PLN) for your foreign currency than you would at other locations.

2. Commission and Fees: Exchange bureaus at airports may charge higher commission fees or service charges for currency exchange transactions. These additional fees can further reduce the amount of cash you receive.

3. Limited Options: At the airport, you may find limited options for currency exchange. There may be only a few exchange booths available, and they might not offer competitive rates due to the captive audience of travelers in need of immediate cash.

4. Alternatives in the City: To get a better exchange rate and lower fees, consider exchanging your currency in the city center of Krakow. There are numerous exchange offices and banks throughout the city that offer competitive rates and lower commission fees.

5. ATMs: Another convenient option for obtaining cash in Krakow is to use ATMs (Automated Teller Machines). ATMs generally offer competitive exchange rates and charge minimal fees. However, be mindful of any fees charged by your own bank for international withdrawals.

6. Prepaid Travel Cards: Prepaid travel cards are another option to consider. These cards allow you to load money onto them before your trip and use them like a debit card while traveling. They often offer competitive exchange rates and may have

lower fees compared to exchanging cash at the airport.
7. Plan Ahead: To avoid the need for immediate cash upon arrival, plan ahead and ensure you have a small amount of local currency with you before departing for Krakow. This can be useful for immediate expenses such as transportation from the airport to your accommodation.

CONCLUSION

Tips for solo travelers, families and LGBTQ + travelers

Krakow is a diverse and welcoming city that caters to various types of travelers. Whether you're a solo traveler, traveling with your family, or identifying as LGBTQ+, here are some tips to enhance your experience in Krakow:

For Solo Travelers:

1. Safety Precautions: As a solo traveler, it's important to prioritize your safety. Stick to well-lit and populated areas, especially at night. Inform someone of your itinerary and stay connected with them. Be cautious of your belongings and avoid displaying expensive items.
2. Join Group Tours or Activities: Participating in group tours or activities can be a great way to meet fellow travelers and engage in shared experiences. Consider joining walking tours, pub crawls, or day trips to explore the city with like-minded individuals.
3. Stay in Social Accommodations: Choose accommodations that offer common areas or host

social events to facilitate interactions with other travelers. Hostels, guesthouses, or social hotels often provide opportunities to meet new people and potentially find travel companions.

For Families:

1. Family-Friendly Attractions: Krakow has plenty of family-friendly attractions to enjoy. Visit the Wawel Castle, the Main Market Square, or the Krakow Zoo. Explore interactive museums like the Museum of Science and Technology or the Ethnographic Museum, which offer educational experiences for all ages.
2. Parks and Playgrounds: Krakow boasts numerous parks and playgrounds where children can run, play, and enjoy the outdoors. Planty Park, Jordan Park, and Park Jordana are some popular options that offer green spaces and recreational facilities.
3. Child-Friendly Restaurants: Look for restaurants that provide kid-friendly menus or have a welcoming atmosphere for families. Many restaurants in Krakow are accommodating to families and offer high chairs, children's menus, and even play areas.

For LGBTQ+ Travelers:

1. LGBTQ+-Friendly Establishments: Krakow has a growing LGBTQ+ scene with LGBTQ+-friendly establishments. Head to the Kazimierz district, which is known for its inclusive atmosphere and vibrant nightlife. You'll find LGBTQ+-friendly bars, clubs, and cafes in this area.
2. LGBTQ+ Events and Festivals: Keep an eye out for LGBTQ+ events and festivals that take place in Krakow throughout the year. These events celebrate diversity and offer a chance to connect with the local LGBTQ+ community and allies.
3. LGBTQ+ Support Organizations: Krakow is home to organizations that provide support and resources for the LGBTQ+ community. Reach out to these organizations for information on LGBTQ+-friendly venues, services, and events happening in the city.

Additional Resources And Contact Information

1. Tourist Information Centers: The Tourist Information Centers in Krakow are a valuable resource for travelers. They provide maps, brochures, and guidance on local attractions, events, and transportation. The main tourist information center is located in the Cloth Hall at

the Main Market Square (Rynek Główny 1/3). Contact: +48 12 354 27 00.

2. Emergency Numbers: In case of emergencies, it's important to know the local emergency contact numbers. The general emergency number in Poland is 112, which can be dialed for police, fire, or medical assistance.

3. Consulates and Embassies: Familiarize yourself with the contact information of your country's consulate or embassy in Poland. They can provide assistance in case of emergencies, lost passports, or other consular services. You can find a list of foreign embassies and consulates in Krakow on the city's official website.

4. Transportation Contacts: Keep the contact information for transportation services readily available. For public transportation, the contact number for the Municipal Transport Authority (MPK Krakow) is +48 703 202 802. For taxi services, reputable companies include Radio Taxi 919 (+48 12 919) and Mega Taxi (+48 12 19626).

5. Health and Medical Services: It's important to have information on healthcare facilities and medical services in Krakow. The emergency medical services number is 112. For non-emergency medical assistance, consult your travel insurance provider for their recommended

healthcare providers or contact your embassy for guidance.

6. Online Resources: Utilize online resources for up-to-date information and travel tips. Visit the official website of the City of Krakow (www.krakow.pl) and the official tourism website (www.krakow.pl/visitkrakow) for comprehensive information on attractions, events, and services. Online travel forums and travel websites can also provide valuable insights from fellow travelers.

7. Local Apps: Consider downloading local apps for transportation, maps, and services. Apps like Jakdojade (public transportation planner), Google Maps, and Uber can assist you in navigating the city and getting around conveniently.

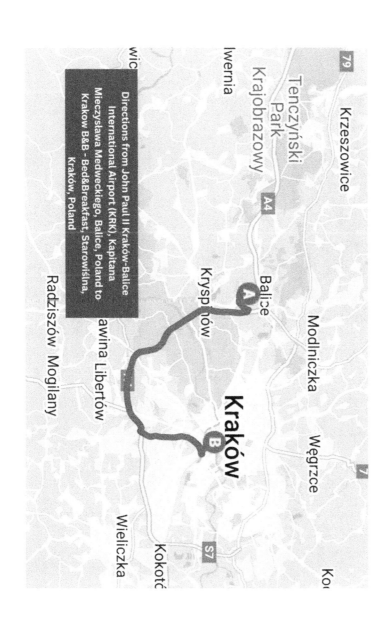

Directions from John Paul II Kraków-Balice
International Airport (KRK), Kapitana
Mieczysława Medweckiego, Balice, Poland to
Krakow B&B - Bed&Breakfast, Starowiślna,
Kraków, Poland

94

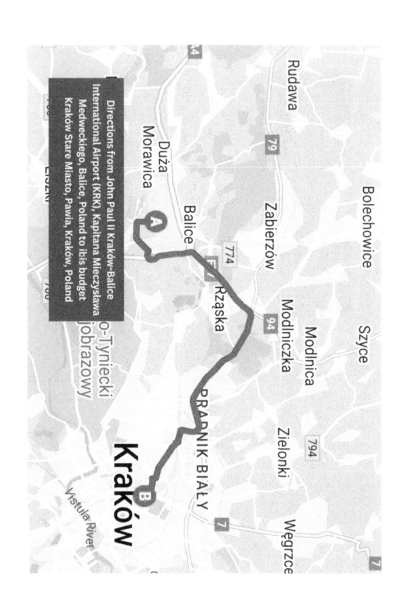

Directions from John Paul II Kraków-Balice International Airport (KRK), Kapitana Mieczysława Medweckiego, Balice, Poland to ibis budget Kraków Stare Miasto, Pawia, Kraków, Poland

95

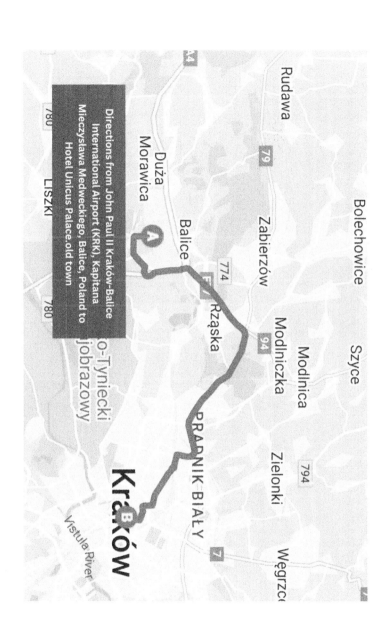

Directions from John Paul II Kraków-Balice
International Airport (KRK), Kapitana
Mieczysława Medweckiego, Balice, Poland to
Hotel Unicus Palace.old town

96

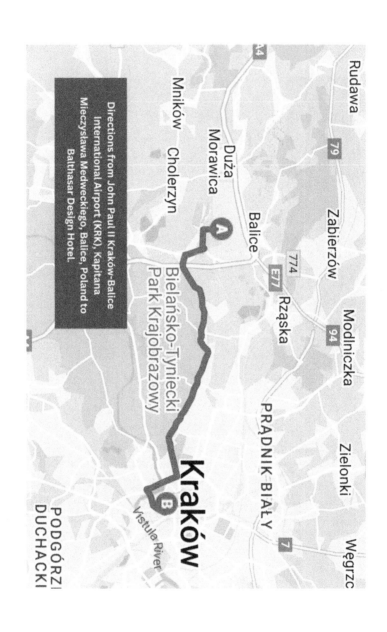

Directions from John Paul II Kraków-Balice International Airport (KRK), Kapitana Mieczysława Medweckiego, Balice, Poland to Balthasar Design Hotel.

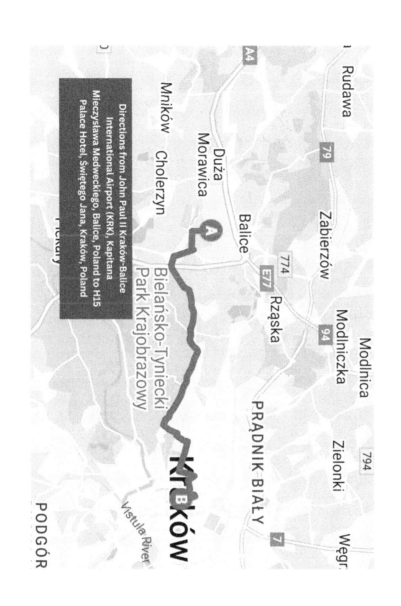

Directions from John Paul II Kraków-Balice
International Airport (KRK), Kapitana
Mieczysława Medweckiego, Balice, Poland to H15
Palace Hotel, Świętego Jana, Kraków, Poland

Mników   Cholerzyn

Duża
Morawica

Balice

Rudawa

A4

79

Zabierzów

774

77 Rząska

Modlniczka

94

Modlnica

Zielonki

794

Węgr.

7

Bielańsko-Tyniecki
Park Krajobrazowy

PRADNIK-BIAŁY

Kraków

Vistula River

PODGÓR

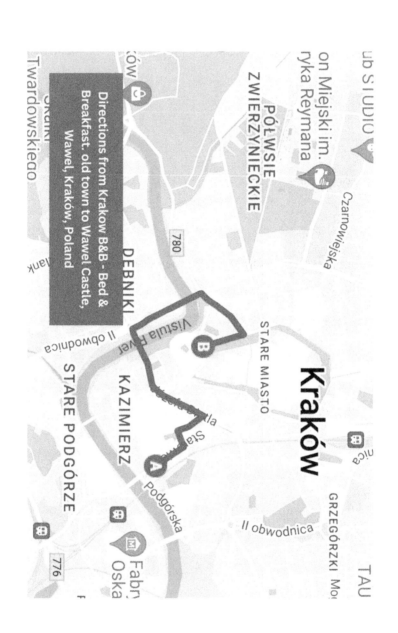

Directions from Krakow B&B - Bed & Breakfast, old town to Wawel Castle, Wawel, Kraków, Poland

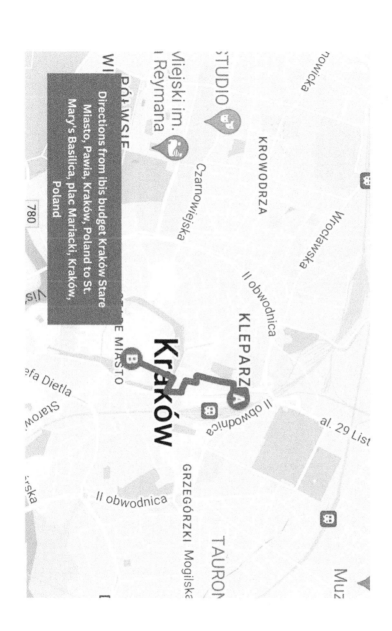

Directions from ibis budget Kraków Stare
Miasto, Pawia, Kraków, Poland to St.
Mary's Basilica, plac Mariacki, Kraków,
Poland

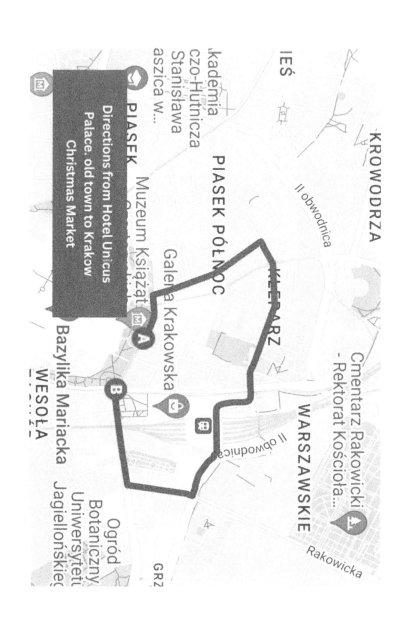

Directions from Hotel Unicus Palace, old town to Krakow Christmas Market

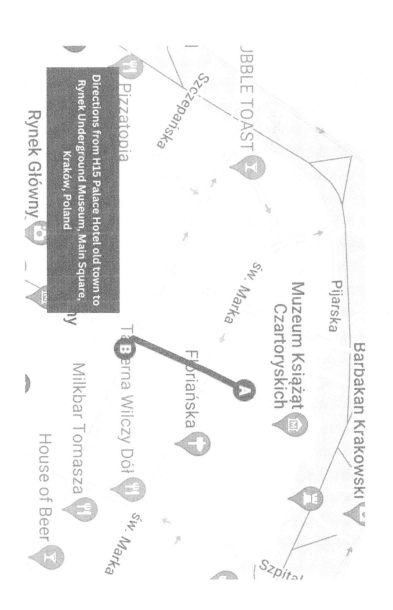

Directions from H15 Palace Hotel old town to Rynek Underground Museum, Main Square, Kraków, Poland

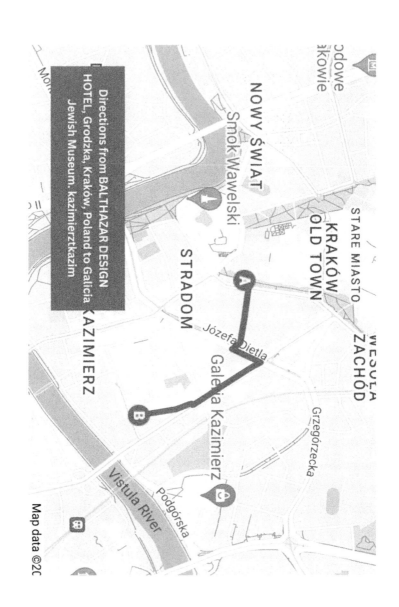

Directions from BALTHAZAR DESIGN
HOTEL, Grodzka, Kraków, Poland to Galicia
Jewish Museum. Kazimierztkazim

Map data ©2C

103

Printed in Great Britain
by Amazon

38853340R00061